Illustrators
Angus McBride/Linden Artists
Richard Hook/Temple Art (*cover*)

First published in 1982 by Macdonald Educational
under the title
Peoples of the Past: Everyday Life in the Seventeenth Century

Reprinted in 1993
by Simon & Schuster Young Books
Campus 400
Maylands Avenue
Hemel Hempstead, Herts HP2 7EZ

© Macdonald Educational Limited, 1982

Photographs
The Art and Architecture Collection 19, 42(T)
Bibliothèque Nationale 8(T), 46(T)
The Bridgeman Art Library/Private Collection 47
British Museum 41
British Tourist Authority 48(TL)
J. Allan Cash 20
Mary Evans Picture Library 55
Fotomas Index 10
Giraudon 8(B), 29, 39, 53(T)
Koninklijk Museum, Antwerp 48(B)
Kunsthistorisches Museum, Vienna 37
The Mansell Collection 54
MAS/Prado 30
The Master and Fellows of Magdalene College,
    Cambridge 12
Mauritshuis, The Hague 17
Metropolitan Museum of Art, New York 46(B)
Museum of London 36

National Maritime Museum 53(B)
The National Trust 48(TR)
Scala/Museum of San Martino, Naples 15
Stadelisches Kunstinstitut, Frankfurt 42(B)

ISBN 0-7500-1469-5

A catalogue record for this book is available from the
    British Library.

Printed and bound in Belgium by Proost International
    Book Production

Everyday Life in
Stuart Times

Laurence Taylor

SIMON & SCHUSTER
YOUNG BOOKS

Contents

Introduction

In the 17th century Europe was sharply divided into two worlds – that of the rich and that of the poor. There was a tiny world of privilege and wealth, and a huge world of poverty and suffering.

But the century was also one of strong religious faith. As in the 16th century, Europe was divided into two opposing religious camps. In the north the Protestant princes wanted to keep the territories and peoples they had won during their struggles with the Roman Catholic rulers. In the south, Roman Catholic countries, such as France, Spain and Austria, wanted to win back the territory lost to the Church. After a long and bitter struggle both sides tired of religious wars and a peace was signed. Yet Europe remained a battlefield for the 'super-powers' of France, Spain and Austria whose kings wanted their countries to grow in power and glory.

It was a century of great artistic achievement. Louis XIV of France attracted all the great painters, sculptors and architects of the time to his palace at Versailles. All over Europe beautiful houses were built and decorated with the work of skilled artists and craftsmen.

Science also flourished. The 17th century is famous for its 'Scientific Revolution'. For centuries men had believed that the earth was the centre of the universe. New discoveries about the universe made it more and more difficult to accept this view. Great scientists like Galileo, Kepler and Newton laid the foundation of modern science and our knowledge of the world.

The rulers

Louis XIV, King of France from 1643 to 1715, was the most powerful ruler in Europe in the 17th century. To show off his power, he had a huge palace built at Versailles. The palace is richly decorated with symbols of the King's power, such as the sun. Louis even called himself *le Roi Soleil*, or 'the Sun King'.

Other European rulers tried to copy Louis. In England King Charles II admired him. But he knew that England could not afford the great palaces and large armies of the powerful French king.

A great king in a splendid palace had to live grandly. Louis followed an elaborate ritual every day. From the moment he was woken in the morning, to the time he went to bed at night, his whole day was organized to impress his subjects.

Many nobles disliked Louis's rituals. But they had to join in or leave the court. Louis was clever. He knew that if the nobles were forced to spend their time and money on

▲ *The young Louis XIV dressed as the sun for a Court masque.*

▲ Louis XIV made his levée (getting up) into an elaborate ceremony. Nobles were specially chosen to attend him. Some only watched. Very favoured ones might be allowed to help Louis dress. The same thing happened when he went to bed.

◄ The splendid palace of Versailles was built for Louis XIV, to display his wealth and power. It is surrounded by enormous formal gardens, with fountains and lakes.

clothes and entertainment, they would not be able to plot against him.

The court at Versailles was very expensive. Louis's constant wars cost thousands of lives and enormous sums of money. By the end of his reign France could no longer afford the glory Louis wanted.

The king's subjects

During the 17th century a new class was growing in society – the middle class. These people were below the king, nobles and gentry, but above the poor. They were either merchants or skilled craftsmen, or members of a profession – law, medicine, the army or the Church. The classes above and below them had a fixed social position, but the middle class did not. A few of its members climbed to the top, married into noble families, and became noble themselves.

Most people, however, were poor. They had to pay heavy taxes to the king and to the Church, and to serve in the army. Although they produced much of the country's wealth, they received few benefits. A few, through hard work and luck, became middle class.

▶ Lesser nobles, gentlemen, army and navy officers
Many of the lesser nobles and gentlemen were landlords, living in the country. The most senior officers in the army and navy (marshals and admirals) were usually great nobles.

◀ *This is the title-page of a book written in 1600. It describes the life of an English gentleman.*

▶ King and queen
Kings and queens were often very powerful. But many European rulers had to face serious rebellions. In England Charles I was beheaded (1649) after a successful rebellion by Parliament.

◀ Thieves and beggars

◀ Labourers, cottagers and paupers
Over half the population belonged to this group.

◀ Farmers and freeholders
These people paid most of the taxes.

◀ Ordinary soldiers and seamen
The lives of these men were harsh, and many more died of hunger and disease than in battle.

◀ Artisans, craftsmen, shopkeepers and merchants
Many were very poor; only a few became as rich as the nobles.

◀ Clergy, doctors, lawyers, artists and scientists
This group grew steadily as demand for their services increased.

▲ Great nobles
In every country rich and powerful men attended the king and queen. Some were given posts in the royal household. Some, including archbishops and bishops, acted as royal advisers.

11

The king's servants

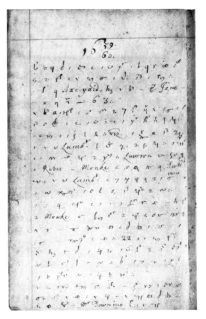

▲ The Englishman, Samuel Pepys (1633–1703), kept a fascinating diary of his life and work. He wrote in a kind of shorthand, so you won't be able to read the page above.

▼ Part of London and the docks before the Fire of London (1666). Near the centre is old St Paul's Cathedral.

At this time kings governed their countries. To help them, they needed ministers who were properly trained, loyal and honest. Members of the king's own family, or of the older nobility, might use their power to plot against him, so kings like Louis XIV chose middle-class men as their ministers. A king also needed a large number of administrators, or civil servants, to carry out his decisions.

In France powerful royal officials called 'intendants' were appointed to do this. Many other kinds of officials were also needed. Judges were appointed to punish wrongdoers. Treasury officials arranged the collection of taxes. Customs officers collected taxes on goods entering and leaving the country.

An English civil servant called Samuel Pepys was in charge of the Navy. Pepys was responsible for organizing and running the dockyards, where ships were built, repaired and prepared for war. He also reformed the Navy, after it had been badly defeated by the Dutch in 1665.

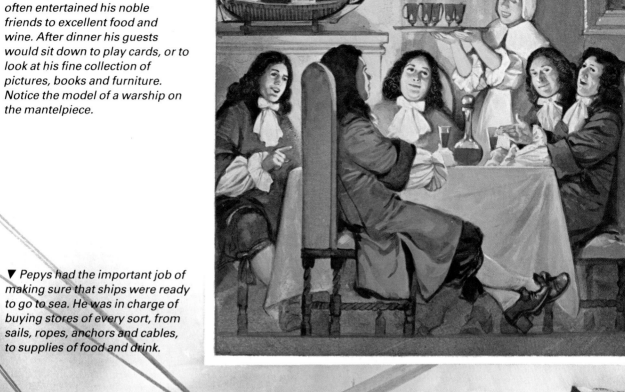

► Pepys lived in a fine house near the Navy Office in London. He often entertained his noble friends to excellent food and wine. After dinner his guests would sit down to play cards, or to look at his fine collection of pictures, books and furniture. Notice the model of a warship on the mantelpiece.

▼ Pepys had the important job of making sure that ships were ready to go to sea. He was in charge of buying stores of every sort, from sails, ropes, anchors and cables, to supplies of food and drink.

Religion, wars and rebellions

There were wars and rebellions almost every year throughout the 17th century. One of the longest and most destructive wars was the 'Thirty Years' War', from 1618 to 1648. It began as a struggle between the Protestants of northern Europe and the Catholics of the south. By 1648 both sides were so war-weary and bankrupt that they made peace.

◀ People were not free to choose what religion they liked. This is an illegal meeting of Puritans, held in a barn, which is being broken up by soldiers.

▼ Soldiers were poorly disciplined, and badly paid and fed. They lived by plundering the country-side, ill-treating and killing those who tried to resist them, and burning their houses.

► This is part of a painting showing a revolt in Naples in 1647. It was led by a fisherman called Masaniello in protest against high taxes.

▼ Sometimes angry peasants hit back at the soldiers. They ambushed small groups of soldiers, and attacked them with farm tools.

Many of the civil wars and rebellions began as struggles between Catholics and Protestants. The Protestant Dutch fought their Catholic Spanish masters for eighty years (1568 to 1648). They wanted to leave the Spanish Empire and become a free Protestant nation. The Catholic Irish bitterly resented their English Protestant overlords. In 1641 they rebelled. In 1649, when the English Civil War was over, Oliver Cromwell went to Ireland to end the rebellion. Cromwell's troops massacred many people.

In France, Louis XIV persecuted the Huguenots, who refused to give up their Protestant beliefs. Finally, in 1685, Louis forced over 200,000 Huguenots to leave France. Many were skilled craftsmen, who were welcomed by other countries.

Disease and medicine

Doctors' cures were often painful, and generally useless. When King Charles II of England fell ill in 1685, twelve doctors treated him. First they took blood from his arm and made him violently sick. Then they shaved his head and applied hot 'potions' to it. This was followed by 'gargles', more blood letting, 'laxatives and medicines'. None of this was any help and after four days Charles died.

Not all doctors were quite so ignorant. One of the most important discoveries in the history of medicine was made by William Harvey, an English doctor. He proved that blood circulates through the body continuously, due to the pumping of the heart. Many doctors refused to accept such discoveries.

Outbreaks of plague occurred throughout Europe during the 17th century. There were outbreaks in London in 1603, 1625 and 1665. The most severe was in 1665, when about 68,000 people died.

Attempts were made to stop the plague spreading. In London, the sick were shut up in their homes for a month and the front door marked with a large red cross. Watchmen stood outside to stop people leaving or entering. The dead had to be buried before sunrise or after sunset, in deep graves; householders had to keep the streets in front of their houses clean; stray dogs were killed, and no pigs or other animals were allowed in the city. The poor suffered most. Their houses were crowded and unhygienic, and disease spread quickly.

▲ Plague is caused by an invisible microbe, which attacks the black rat. Fleas live on the rat, and carry the disease to human beings by biting them. In the 17th century doctors and scientists did not know this.

▼ The plague struck suddenly, and affected thousands. Whole families died, shut up in their homes.

▼ Red crosses were painted on the doors of houses where plague had struck as a warning to passers-by.

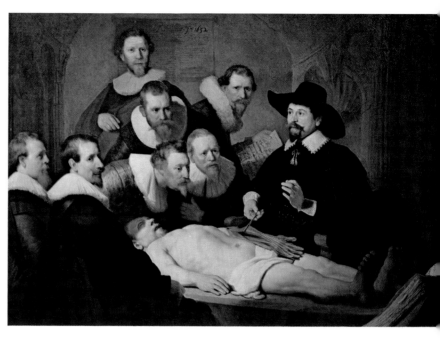

◀ Doctors tried to protect themselves against the disease. They wore long leather coats with hoods and gloves. The mask was stuffed with herbs, and the 'eyes' were made of glass.

▲ Rembrandt painted The Anatomy Lesson in 1632. A doctor is dissecting a body in front of students. Everyone wears ordinary clothes, since nothing was known about germs.

▼ When plague broke out wealthy people fled from the city. Many left by boat for the country.

▼ The dead were buried at night or early in the morning, when few people were about.

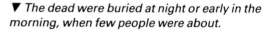

▼ The poor left on foot or by cart. They were often turned away by villagers fearing the plague.

▼ So many people died that great pits were dug to bury the bodies together.

The Great Fire of London

In 1665 and 1666 two disasters struck London. The plague of 1665 was followed by a great fire. It started in a bakery in Pudding Lane, near London Bridge, on 2 September 1666.

At first people living a little way away were not worried. Samuel Pepys wrote in his *Diary* that his maid, Jane 'called us up about three in the morning, to tell us of a great fire in the City. So I rose . . . and went to her window . . . I thought it far enough off and so went to bed again to sleep'. But when Pepys woke later that morning, it was still burning.

▼ As the fire spread through the narrow streets of the crowded city there was total panic. People struggled and fought to escape to safety across the river. The noise of the flames, the thick smoke and confusion was even more terrifying at night.

► One of the buildings burnt down by the Great Fire was St Paul's Cathedral. This is the one which was built to replace it. It was designed by Sir Christopher Wren. He also designed many smaller churches and other buildings to replace those destroyed by the fire.

Later in the day Charles II ordered that houses in the fire's path should be pulled down or blown up. But still the fire spread. By Monday, 3 September, it had reached the centre of the City. Everywhere there was panic. The streets were jammed with people trying to escape, pushing handcarts and barrows, heaped with their belongings. Even the Thames was packed with traffic, as boats ferried frightened people to safety on the south bank.

Four days later the fire had died down. It had destroyed over 13,000 houses and 87 churches, and had made thousands homeless.

But the Great Fire did some good. It must have killed the rats which carried the plague fleas, for London never suffered another outbreak of the plague.

Law and order

▲ The corpses of thieves and robbers were left hanging in public places. These are the gallows at Inkpen Common, Berkshire.

In 1630, in Milan, Italy, two men were accused of daubing someone's wall with cow-dung. They were tortured and confessed. They were ordered to be taken to the place of execution in a cart, their bodies struck with red-hot pokers as the cart moved through the streets, their hands chopped off, their bodies broken on the rack, their throats cut and their corpses burnt. In many countries nearly every crime was punished by death. Men, women and children regularly went to watch these executions.

In the past, crime had been easier to deal with because towns and villages were smaller. Where everyone knew everybody else, it was easier to track down wrongdoers. However, as towns and cities grew, so did the number of criminals. Streets were poorly lit and there were no proper police forces. Severe punishments were thought to be the only way to stop crime.

Crimes were dealt with at several levels. The most serious ones, such as treason or rebellion, went to the court of the King's Bench (left). The Quarter Sessions (below left) dealt with all serious crimes except ones with a death penalty. The local Justices of the Peace met four times a year to try those cases. They were advised by a trained Clerk of the Peace, who sat below them. Each district had a Justice of the Peace (below). He dealt with some crimes in his own house.

In lonely parts of the countryside even large groups of travellers were not safe. Waggon trains were often attacked by gangs of disbanded soldiers.

The narrow, badly-lit streets of towns were especially dangerous at night. There were few watchmen, and muggings were common.

The changing landscape

1

2

3

As the population of Europe grew, more food, clothing, fuel and shelter were needed. To meet these needs land was cleared to grow more crops and graze more animals. Farmers also tried to produce more food from the same area of land.

Northern Europe had many woods and forests. Clearing them was an easy way to get more farm land. The trees provided fuel and wood for making things.

In parts of Europe low-lying, marshy areas were drained. This was expensive, but the new land produced good crops.

Another way to get more land was by 'enclosure'. This meant surrounding (or enclosing) land with ditches or hedges. In most villages three kinds of land could be enclosed: the scrubby waste land outside the village, where the villagers collected wood for fuel; the common land, where they grazed their cows, sheep and geese; or their strips of land in the great open fields.

Only wealthy landowners could afford enclosure. Sometimes they paid the village farmers for the land they were taking away. At other times the landowners used force, and there were fierce battles as the villagers fought to protect their rights.

▲ Three stages in making charcoal. Charcoal, made from wood, was essential for making iron.
1. A round area was cleared and a pole put up in the centre.
2. The wood was arranged in a round stack, 3 metres high.
3. Turf was put on the outside. The stack burned slowly for 5 or 6 days.

► In many parts of the country landlords and village farmers stuck to the old farming methods. Corn and other crops were grown on narrow strips in open fields. Animals were grazed on the village meadows and surrounding commonland.

▲ Reclaimed farmland in the Netherlands. This was a low-lying area in the north of Europe. The land was often flooded by the sea, so the Dutch became skilled at draining and building dykes to keep the sea back. Windmills helped to pump the water away.

◀ Where the demand for corn, butter, milk and meat was growing, customs began to change. In this village the landlord and farmers have agreed to enclose the land. This will make larger fields, and improve the crops. What other changes can you see?

The farming year

► Winter
At this time of year the weather prevents work in the fields. But there is still plenty to do.

► Autumn
In southern Europe this is the time of the wine harvest, when the ripe grapes are picked and trampled to make wine. In other parts of Europe apples, pears and other fruits are picked and stored.

◄ Spring
This is a season of great activity. Animals are put out to fresh pasture, and shepherds are busy lambing. Fields are ploughed and sown. Children scare birds away from the seeds.

◄ Summer
Everybody helps with the harvest. The men cut the corn, the women and children tie it into sheaves to dry. A good harvest calls for great celebration.

25

Country gentlemen

Most of the countryside belonged to three kinds of people: kings, nobles and gentlemen.

In almost every parish there was at least one gentleman, descended from an old noble family. During the late 16th and early 17th centuries many gentlemen rebuilt their semi-fortified houses. They added rooms, larger windows and more comfortable furniture. There were gardens and lawns in front of the house. Beyond was parkland in which cattle and sheep grazed.

Close to the house was a sunny, walled kitchen garden. Nearby was the home farm. This provided meat, eggs, milk, cheese and butter for the gentleman's household.

Unlike people below them in social rank, gentlemen and their families did not have to work with their hands. They paid servants to work for them.

Together, the gentlemen and the nobles formed a rich and powerful group. Most people below them worked for them and so depended on them.

▶ *All over Europe nobles and gentlemen were building new, grander and more luxurious houses on their country estates. This is the first Eaton Hall in Cheshire, which was built at the end of the 17th century.*

▼ *Three European gentlemen in typical 17th-century dress 1. An English gentleman 2. A French seigneur 3. A Spanish hidalgo.*

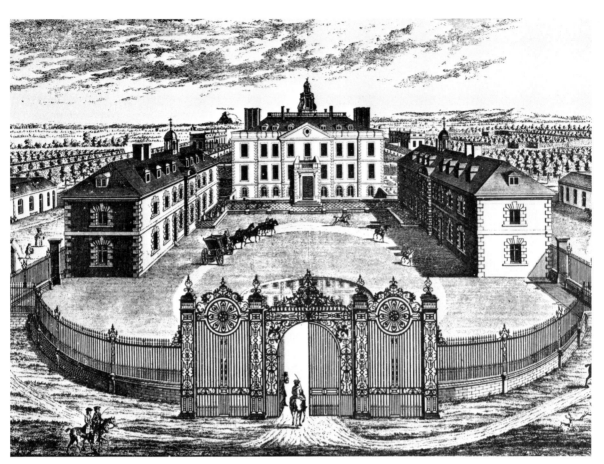

▼ When they were not dealing with estate business, or upholding law and order, gentlemen enjoyed hunting, fishing and shooting.

A peasant's life

A peasant's life was short and hard. Both men and women had to work every day, all day, and most people died before they were 40.

Peasants did not own land. Sometimes, as in England, they paid rent to the landowner for farming part of his land. In France, some peasants were *metayers*. The landowner gave them land, seed, animals and tools. In return, at harvest time, they had to give him half, or more, of what they had grown that year. The poorest peasants were day labourers. They had to find work every day, and were paid very little.

The main cause of the peasants' suffering was high taxation. There were many different taxes: taxes paid to the Church, taxes paid to the local lord, and, in France, a tax for using salt.

Some peasants did not farm, but had a trade. Most villages had a blacksmith and a wheelwright. In areas where cloth was made, many people also worked as spinners or weavers. They had more money than many peasant farmers. They had enough to eat, some furniture, a proper cottage, and some good clothes to wear on feastdays. But the poorer peasants lived miserably, especially in times of famine or war.

▶ Poor peasant farmers, and their even poorer labourers, got up at dawn (1). They worked all day in the fields (2) and came wearily home at sunset (3).

Their homes were tumbledown and damp (4). They had very little furniture. Poor farmers had to give much of what they grew as rent to the local lord (5). Besides this they had to pay a tenth (tithe) of their produce of corn, wine, eggs and cheese to the local church (6).

In the evenings poor families gathered round the fire for warmth (7). They ate soup and bread most of the time.

▼ Woollen cloth was England's biggest export in the 17th century. Most weavers worked in their own cottages.

The woollen thread was brought to the weavers by middlemen, who came back to collect the cloth. The middlemen worked for wealthy merchants who sold the finished cloth for much more than they paid the weavers.

1

2

3

4

5

6

7

▼ This painting shows a baker's family in a small French town. In the country people usually baked their own bread, but in towns people often bought it from a baker. They could also take food, such as meat, to be cooked for them in the baker's oven.

Growing up

In the 17th century nearly half the population of Europe was less than sixteen years old. This was because people died young. Schools were expensive, so only tradesmen and wealthy farmers could afford to send their sons to school. The very rich paid tutors to teach their children at home. Schools were rough, and children were severely punished for giving wrong answers or misbehaving. The main subjects were Latin, Greek and religious instruction.

Few girls went to school. They were trained to become housewives. Older girls had to look after younger children, and help with all the household tasks, such as cooking, cleaning, mending and spinning. Boys helped their fathers, and so learned jobs such as ploughing, baking, weaving, shoeing horses or milling corn. They had to work long hours, like their parents.

Poor children were often sent away to work for wealthier families when they were eleven or twelve. Girls were trained as servants in the house, and boys as outdoor servants, such as stable-boys.

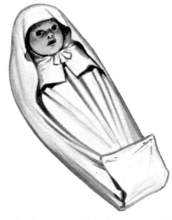

▲ *Babies were tightly wrapped in swaddling clothes. They slept in cradles like the one below.*

▼ *A walking frame on wheels, very like ones used today.*

◄ *Margarita Teresa, daughter of Philip IV of Spain, in 1656. She is wearing clothes like those of the adults.*

Rocking horse

Toy gun

◄Some 17th-century toys.

Doll

▶ A young boy, wearing a dress.
Boys and girls wore the same
clothes till they were about six.
Then boys were breeched (put
into breeches). The father's
clothes were fashionable in 1640.

▼ Children learned their letters
from a horn book like this. The
letters are protected with a piece
of transparent horn.

▼ Many charity schools for poor
boys and girls were founded at
the end of the 17th century.

ABCDEFG
HIJKLMN
OPQRST
VUWXYZ
abcdefghij
klmnopqrís
tvuwxyz&
·A·E·I·O·U·Y

Costume and fashion

Poor children wore plain, hard-wearing clothes, very like those worn by their parents and grandparents. Their few clothes had to last for a long time. Finer clothes were handed down from one generation to another. They were only worn on holidays. A man might own one hat, a doublet, a pair of leather breeches, a pair of woollen breeches, a jerkin, two shirts and two pairs of shoes. The very poor might just wear a long woollen or linen shirt, with leather sandals.

Rich people had far more clothes, and their styles often changed. Expensive jewellery and fashionable clothes showed how rich people were. Even fashionable people smelled strongly because soap was expensive.

Traders brought new materials, such as muslin and cotton, from abroad. Styles changed faster and faster. By the end of the century men were wearing wide, floppy hats, high-heeled boots, enormous wigs, and breeches covered with ribbons. Women wore make-up and tight corsets to make their waists small.

▼ Fashionable ladies wore elaborate make-up. Their hair was curled, and parted in the middle. This style was brought to England by Charles I's French wife, Henrietta Maria. Some ladies shaved off their eyebrows, and stuck on false ones made of mouse-skin! There was also a fashion for patches – fancy shapes cut out of black paper and stuck on to the face.

▼ Beggar dressed in rags with bare feet.

▲ Fashion in 1640. The man wears a high-fitting doublet, knee breeches, ruffled shirt-sleeves and a wide brimmed hat and plume. The lady's dress is high-waisted, with a low-necked bodice, trailing gown and full sleeves.

▼ Street scene at the end of the 17th century. The man is most fashionable, with his huge hat, large wig and lace cravat. His breeches are very elaborate.

▲ Puritans were strict Protestants, who believed that people should live simply. They disapproved of fashion, and wore plain, dark clothes.

Food and drink

For many people, food became better in the 17th century. The poor still lived mainly on bread and beer, but they ate meat (usually bacon) and cheese more often. In southern Europe wine, not beer, was the main drink.

Richer people ate enormous amounts of meat, although vegetables were still unpopular. Table manners were improving, and people used forks and spoons as well as knives. Poor people still ate off pewter or wooden plates, on a bare table. The rich now used china and glass, and covered their tables with linen cloths.

Explorers brought new foods back from abroad. Potatoes, from South America, had become common by the end of the 17th century. They were a useful alternative to bread when grain was expensive.

The explorers also brought new drinks to Europe. At first only rich people could afford tea, coffee and chocolate (made from cacao). But prices fell as more of these were grown. By the end of the century tea- and coffee-drinking were common and coffee-houses became popular meeting-places in many towns and cities.

▲ A 'blackjack' (beer-jug) and mug. They were made of leather. The leather was softened in water, then shaped round a wooden block and sewn. It was set hard by boiling.

▶ The dinner which Samuel Pepys served one day included two neats' tongues (ox tongues) and tanzy (a kind of pudding).

Carp

Salmon

Tanzy

Chickens

Neats' tongues

Cheese

▲ Wealthier families ate sitting at a simple table, made of long wooden boards. At meal-times this was covered with a white cloth. There was a lot of food, but few plates and dishes. Several courses were eaten off the same plate. Many people used only spoons and knives, but forks were becoming more common.

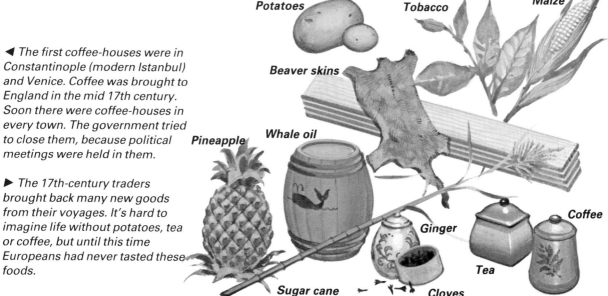

Potatoes

Tobacco

Maize

Beaver skins

◀ The first coffee-houses were in Constantinople (modern Istanbul) and Venice. Coffee was brought to England in the mid 17th century. Soon there were coffee-houses in every town. The government tried to close them, because political meetings were held in them.

▶ The 17th-century traders brought back many new goods from their voyages. It's hard to imagine life without potatoes, tea or coffee, but until this time Europeans had never tasted these foods.

Pineapple

Whale oil

Ginger

Coffee

Tea

Sugar cane

Cloves

Holy days and holidays

The great holiday of the year was called Carnival. This was the season from December to Lent, the time of fasting before Easter. During Carnival the poor could make fun of their betters without being punished. Everyone ate and drank enormously, and paraded through the streets in strange or ridiculous costumes.

There were other important festivals. On the first of May, to celebrate the coming of Spring, there were noisy games, and people danced around the maypole. Another festival was at harvest time, when feasting and dancing were followed by services of thanksgiving in churches.

Sports were part of holidays. Crowds flocked to see bears, bulls and boars being 'baited', snapped at by dogs. Cockfights were very popular. Less cruel were running, jumping and wrestling contests.

In England, men and boys played football on Sunday afternoon. The ball was a blown-up pig's bladder. There were many players on each side, and the game often became a fight. Then, order had to be restored by the parish constable, or town watchman.

▼ When the Thames froze over during the winter of 1683–84, a frost fair was held on the ice. Visitors from the country found it an extraordinary sight. The ice was so thick that fires could be lit on it!

► Happy peasants dancing at a village fair, painted by the Flemish artist Pieter Bruegel. Fairs were held on feastdays and holy days, such as Easter. They gave people a chance to relax and enjoy themselves.

◄ Cockfighting was a cruel sport. Sharp spurs were tied on to the birds' legs, and they fought to the death. The spectators laid bets on which bird would win.

▼ Wearing masks was part of the fun of Carnival. No-one knew who was who. The hobbyhorse was rather a scary figure at Carnival, chasing people up the narrow alleys.

Entertainment for the rich

A favourite pastime of kings and their courts was hunting stags, wild boar and wolves. After a hunt there was often a lavish ball or other entertainment. Gambling was very popular, particularly at Versailles, which was nicknamed 'the gambling den'. Louis XIV disliked playing cards; he preferred billiards.

The theatre was very fashionable, so nobles paid large sums of money to have their own boxes. There they played cards before and after the performances.

Beneath the constant pleasure-seeking there was another, more desperate, side to the life of the rich. They had to seek the king's favour all the time, so there was fierce rivalry among them. This often led to pointless quarrels, which were settled by duels, usually with swords. Duels frequently ended in serious wounds and sometimes even in death.

▲ In pellmell players tried to hit a wooden ball through a hanging iron ring.

▼ A stag hunt arranged for the ladies of the Spanish court. The animals are driven into a trap, and then killed.

◄ Masques, balls and dancing were very popular with the nobles at court. The man and woman in front are about to lead a dance.

▼ Some pastimes of the wealthy. Many gentlemen (1) enjoyed fishing.

Billiards (2) was played with curved cues.

Most people could play an instrument, or sing (3).

Duelling (4) was discouraged. But it was still a common way to settle an argument.

1

2

3

4

The growing cities

Cities like London, Lisbon, Seville and Amsterdam grew fast because they were on the main sea trade routes. Amsterdam was the wealthiest trading city. During the early 17th century more canals were dug, so ships could sail right into the city. The land between the canals was sold to merchants who built houses and warehouses along the canals. The city became known as the 'Venice of the North'.

Other cities, like Madrid, Vienna and Rome, grew because they were the centres of great empires. Rome contained the Vatican, which was the heart of the Roman Catholic Church. An enormous new church, St Peter's, was built there. It was meant to show the power of the Pope, the head of the Roman Catholic Church.

London was one of the busiest and most crowded cities in Europe. The destruction caused by the Great Fire of 1666 meant that much of the city could be redesigned and rebuilt. Streets were widened, and new buildings could not be above a certain height. But London soon began to sprawl in all directions.

▼ Amsterdam was a port, and its canal system was enlarged in the 17th century. This allowed ships to sail into the city.

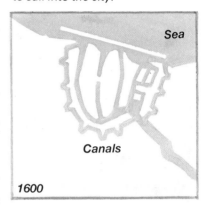

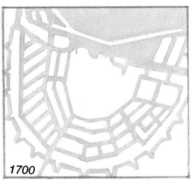

▼ This is the old London Bridge, which was burnt down in the Great Fire of London.

▲ In 1655 Gianlorenzo Bernini was commissioned by Pope Alexander VII to build a piazza in front of St Peter's. He designed one of the most exciting and dramatic sights in Europe.

Merchants and bankers

▼ Vaux-le-Vicomte, the splendid
château built for Nicholas
Fouquet. It probably gave Louis
XIV the idea for Versailles.

Until the 17th century the nobles were the most important people after the king. Now groups of rich, powerful merchants began to challenge the nobles. The merchants were important because they owned the ships which brought goods from all over the world to Europe. They also controlled buying, selling and transport, and owned the workshops where goods were made.

Successful merchants became rich. Some stopped trading and concentrated on lending money. They became bankers. Kings and nobles had to borrow money from them, so the bankers became very powerful. Some were employed by rulers to help collect taxes. Nicholas Fouquet, a French banker employed by Louis XIV, became so rich he built a magnificent château at Vaux-le-Vicomte. In 1661 Louis XIV was invited to a house-warming there. Louis was so jealous of Fouquet's grand house that he had him arrested!

▼ By the 17th century the great merchants of Europe were trading to all parts of the known world. They became bankers as well as traders. The coat of arms (above) was used by the East India Company, a group of wealthy English traders.

◄ As trade grew 'exchanges' were built. Here merchants met and dealt in various goods. This exchange was built in Amsterdam. Merchants from all over Europe met here to deal in goods from the Dutch East Indies.

43

Craftsmen and workers

▼ Most goods were made and repaired by hand, by craftsmen. You would find all these people in any town.

▲ Making clothes was a slow job. The poor could not afford to buy fashionable and expensive clothes.

▲ Saddlers made and repaired harnesses and saddles. Horses were used for most forms of transport.

▲ You could not buy shoes ready-made. The shoemaker measured your feet, then made a pair of shoes to fit you.

▲ Wheelwrights made wheels for carts and coaches. Here one man is using a spokeshave to shape a spoke. Another is using a hand-drill, to make a hole to fit the axle.

▲ The knife-grinder (right) sharpened knives. He called at houses, and worked in the street.

▶ Goldsmiths usually worked together, in workshops like this. Apprentices worked for several years before they became skilled craftsmen.

44

There were no factories in the 17th century. Everything was made by hand, by thousands of craftsmen and less skilled workers.

Many were carpenters of some sort. Wood was used to make the framework of houses, and often the whole building. It was used to make ships and coaches, wheels and furniture, and even the machinery in windmills and watermills.

Cloth-making also employed thousands of people throughout Europe. The raw materials were usually wool, flax or silk, although cotton was beginning to be imported from abroad. Spinning and weaving were done by workers in their own homes; spinning was done by women and children and weaving by men. The cloth they made was sent to other skilled workers who dyed and finished it.

The skilled craftsmen who made luxury goods for the rich usually lived in towns and cities. They worked in workshops, like the famous glassworks of Venice, or the goldsmiths and silversmiths in Florence. The master craftsmen who owned these workshops employed a small number of workmen to help them. They usually served a seven-year apprenticeship to learn their trade.

▲ Town criers shouted out local news, and told people when events were happening.

▲ People entertained themselves by singing popular songs. Song sheets were sold by street-sellers.

▲ The ratcatcher carried a sign like this, to tell people what he did.

▲ Porters carried goods, because many streets were too narrow for carts.

▲ Small boys were employed by chimney sweeps to climb and clean chimneys.

The poor

Poverty was a great problem in 17th-century Europe. The population was growing very fast, and there was not enough work for everyone. Poor people wandered the countryside and towns, living by begging and stealing. Some were too ill or weak to work; others were fit, but could not find work.

Beggars were cruelly treated. In England they were often whipped out of the parish and sent back to where they had come from. Some parishes put the poor into workhouses, which were more like prisons. This happened in France as well.

When trade was bad thousands of workers in the cloth industry lost their jobs. Suddenly there would be far more hungry, desperate people moving around Europe. Famines made the problem worse, and there were often riots. To deal with this, some authorities gave food and clothes to the poor. Others treated the poor even more cruelly than before in an effort to get rid of them.

Sometimes wealthy people tried to help. They built almshouses, or they gave food and clothes to the poor on their land. But most poor people were not helped, and the problem of poverty remained.

▲ There was a serious famine in France in 1693. The rich queued for bread, but the poor starved.

◀ When harvests failed the price of bread rose. Poor people came to town to beg. Bread was a major part of their diet.

▼ Many people wandered the country, like these Italian gypsies. They carried with them all that they owned.

▲ Wealthy people often left money in their wills to build almshouses, in which old men and women could live free.

▼ This is part of a painting called The Tichborne Dole. It shows a wealthy family giving food to the poor people of Tichborne.

Homes and gardens

A new style of building became popular during the 17th century. English architects, such as Inigo Jones, were influenced by the work of the great 16th-century Italian architects. Instead of Elizabethan 'E'-shaped mansions they designed houses that were more box-like, with sloping roofs and plain rectangular windows. Inside, the rooms were small and regular.

The rich planted formal gardens round their new houses. Flower gardens were arranged in rectangles and squares, divided by broad walks, and often had a sundial in the centre. Box or lavender hedges were trimmed into ornamental shapes, or planted as mazes.

Gardening was made popular in England by Protestants fleeing from the religious wars in the Netherlands in the 1560s. They brought many new plants, such as tulips, laburnum, nasturtiums and love-in-the-mist.

By the end of the century more natural gardens were becoming popular. This was the beginning of landscape gardening.

▲ *Three kinds of 17th-century chair.*

▼ *The plan of a prosperous farmer's house, taken from an inventory made after his death in 1608. The inventory listed everything he owned and what it was worth.*

1. Hall
2. Parlour
3. Room over parlour
4. Kitchen
5. Buttery entry
6. Dairy
7. Room over hall
8. Buttery
9. Maid's room
10. Room over entry
11. Cheese room
12. Granary

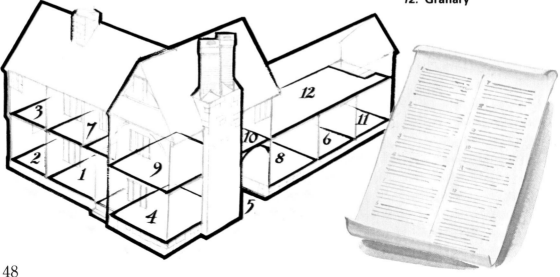

▲ The Englishman Grinling Gibbons was a wonderfully skilled woodcarver. His delicate wood carvings of fruit and flowers look very realistic. They delighted Charles II, who became one of his patrons.

▼ At the beginning of the 17th century gardens were still very formal. This French painting shows the activities in a large garden in spring. You can see that the flowerbeds are arranged in a geometric pattern, divided by low hedges.

▲ The Queen's House at Greenwich was designed by Inigo Jones and built between 1616 and 1635. Its clear-cut outline and beautiful proportions brought the style of Italian Renaissance building to England.

Travel and communication

Few people travelled for pleasure. Travel was slow, uncomfortable and often dangerous. In bad weather rivers could sweep away bridges, halt ferries and turn roads into swamps. Snowstorms and snowdrifts could block roads for days, even weeks. Robbers were a constant threat.

The most common form of transport was on horseback. Poor people walked, or travelled in goods waggons. These were huge and heavy. Each was drawn by a team of up to twelve horses, and rarely went faster than walking speed. Stage-coaches were expensive and uncomfortable. Only the rich could afford to use them. The fastest means of transport was the letter-post. But even this varied with the weather. The postal service across Europe, from Lisbon in Portugal to Danzig on the Baltic coast, could take between 13 and 53 days to cover 3200 kilometres.

▲ In the 1640s it took ten days to send letters from London to Edinburgh by mounted post boy. The cost depended on the number of pages sent.

▼ Travellers had to pay a toll when they crossed someone's land. The tolls were collected at tollgates, like this one. The tollgate-keeper lived in the house next to the tollgate.

◄ *This is a litter. It was either carried by men or had a horse at the front and back. It had a light wooden framework covered with leather. The traveller sat inside.*

▲ *Only rich families could afford to keep a coach, horses and driver. The windows had no glass, and there were few springs so a coach journey was uncomfortable.*

▲ *Many goods were carried on open carts like this one. They were pulled by strong farmhorses and led by a carter.*

▲ *Some pack-horses, laden with goods, are crossing a bridge. One barge is carrying coals. The 'tilt boat', with a canopy, carries passengers.*

▼ *This is a stage waggon, for passengers. It was an ordinary cart, covered with cloth to keep the rain out. A heavy load could need up to six horses.*

Machines and inventions

◀ Guns became safer, faster and more accurate in the 17th century. This is a flintlock pistol. The flintlock firing mechanism was safer than the matchlock (above) and gradually replaced it.

Several 17th-century inventions helped make machines more powerful and efficient.

A new type of mill was designed. This was the tower-mill, which gave more power than the old post-mill. In the new mills only the top, to which the sails were attached, moved. As the machinery did not move with the sails, much more powerful mills could be built. They were used to grind corn, pump water, crush seed for oil, make gunpowder and pulp rags into paper.

Water-power was also improved. Water-wheels were used for splitting iron rods, working hammers in forges and machinery in silk mills.

Industries such as clockmaking and printing were improved. In the past, one skilled craftsman had made a clock or book. Now the process was divided into many different tasks. Each workman did one task, such as making the type, typesetting, printing or binding the book. It took less time to make each book, so more could be made.

Guns were made more precisely and became more accurate. This was to change warfare completely.

▲ As the houses of the wealthy held more and more precious objects, they had to be protected. Ingenious and highly decorated locks like this one, were made.

► The waterworks at Marly-sur-Seine. This was the biggest waterwheel machine ever made. It was built for Louis XIV, to supply the fountains at the palace of Versailles.

▼ A travelling clock. It had a special balance-wheel so that it would keep time even when moving.

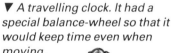

► The first Eddystone lighthouse, built at the end of the 17th century. It was destroyed in a great storm in 1703.

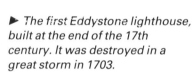

▼ The 'Sovereign of the Seas' was built in 1637, in England. The Dutch called the ship the 'Golden Devil', because there was so much carving and gilding on the stern.

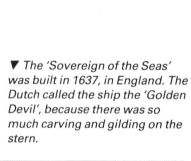

Scientific advances

▼ This detailed drawing of a flea comes from a book called Micrographia by the 17th-century scientist Robert Hooke. He made his own microscope (below) and drew what he saw through it. His book was the first written about using microscopes.

Hooke was one of the founding members of the Royal Society. This was a group of men who met to hear scientific lectures. Some other famous members were Sir Christopher Wren, Sir Isaac Newton, Samuel Pepys, the chemist Robert Boyle, and John Evelyn, another diarist.

During the 17th century people gradually realized that the old superstitious explanations of the world did not fit the facts that were being discovered about it. Many of the new discoveries were different from the Church's view of the world. Because of this, scientists were attacked by the Church. For example, the Italian astronomer Galileo said that the earth went round the sun, not the other way round. In 1633 he was placed under house arrest for the rest of his life, and prevented from publishing his ideas.

Although the Church silenced some scientists, it could not stop the advance of science. Among the men whose discoveries transformed scientific knowledge were astronomers like the German Johann Kepler and the Dane Tycho Brahe, and mathematicians like the Frenchmen Rene Descartes and Blaise Pascal.

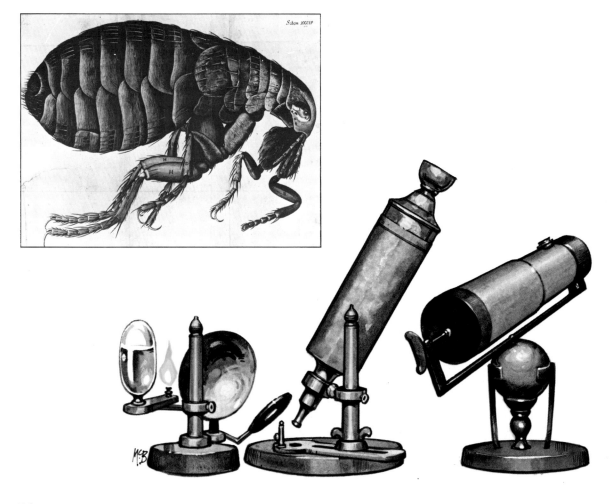

◄ This is the first steam engine designed by Thomas Savery in 1698. It was used for pumping water out of mines. This meant that mine shafts could be dug much deeper, without being flooded.

1. Steam enters the container A. Water is displaced up through valves B.
2. When all the water has left A, steam stops coming in. Cold water is poured on to A from the cistern C.
3. The cold water condenses the steam in A. This creates a vacuum, drawing water up through the pipe D, through the valves B.
The same process happens in the other container E, while A is cooling.

THE OLD OBSERVING-ROOM, GREENWICH.

◄ Astronomy became a science in the 17th century. Stronger, more accurate telescopes meant that astronomers could make exact observations. This is the Royal Observatory at Greenwich in London.

Europe overseas

▼ *Most European settlements in America were near the coast or in river valleys. This was because it was difficult and dangerous to travel overland. The foreign explorers and settlers claimed land which was not theirs, so they had to fight the native people all the time.*

By the end of the 17th century Europe had links with most of the known world. In South and Central America the Spanish and Portuguese made enormous conquests. The Dutch had trading posts in the East Indies. Britain and France struggled to establish settlements in North America and trading posts in India. Many young men went to these colonies to make their fortunes. Land was cheap, and so were people to work on it.

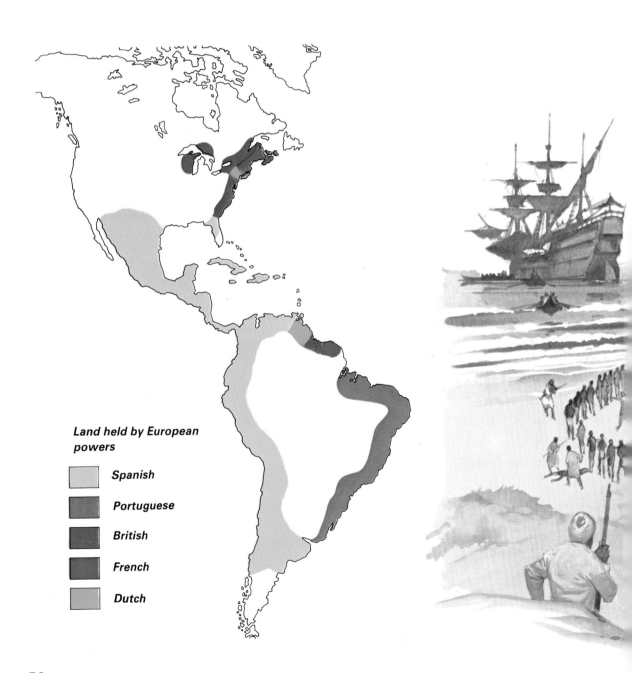

Land held by European powers

- Spanish
- Portuguese
- British
- French
- Dutch

▲ A fort in New England being attacked by Indians. There were many wars between the settlers and the Indians, whose land they took.

European countries now ruled over peoples of many different races and religions. These people were often forced to adopt the language, customs and religion of their European rulers.

Many of these peoples were badly treated, because the Europeans regarded them as inferior. They had to work long hours in gold and silver mines, or on plantations. Slaves, brought from Africa, were treated no better than cattle.

▼ Arab slave traders in West Africa, selling slaves to an English captain, who will sell them to settlers in the New World. There they will work on the plantations.

Main events

1600 The English East India Company was founded.

1603 Elizabeth I of England died. James VI of Scotland, the son of Mary Queen of Scots, became King James I of England.

1605 Catholic plotters, led by Guy Fawkes, tried to blow up the Houses of Parliament. They failed.

1607 One hundred and four Englishmen established the first permanent English settlement in North America at Jamestown, Virginia.

1609 A twelve years' truce was signed between the Spaniards and their rebellious Dutch subjects.

1618 The beginning of the 30 Years' War which was to involve almost every country in Europe.

1620 The Pilgrim Fathers sailed across the Atlantic in the *Mayflower* and settled in Plymouth, Massachusetts.

1624 Richelieu, one of the most famous of all French ministers, joined King Louis XIII's Council.

1625 James I died and was succeeded by his eldest son Charles I. Both kings faced great hostility from Parliament.

1628 In France Huguenot (Protestant) rebels were defeated by Richelieu at La Rochelle.

1629 Charles I dissolved Parliament. For eleven years the King tried to rule the country without Parliament.

1630 English Puritans (extreme Protestants) who disagreed with Charles I, began a migration to North America. By 1643 some 65,000 had left the country.

1641 A savage civil war started in Ireland. The Catholics struggled to drive out their English Protestant landlords.

1641 The English Parliament, which had been recalled by Charles, ordered the execution of his chief minister the Earl of Strafford.

1642 The start of the English Civil War.

1643 Louis XIII of France died. Ann of Austria, his widow, became regent as Louis XIV, her son, was still a child.

1645 Battle of Naseby. The Royalist Army was finally defeated by the armies of Parliament.

1646 The end of the English Civil War. Charles I escaped to Scotland, but was later handed back to the Parliamentary Army.

1648 The Treaty of Westphalia ended the 30 Years' War in Europe.
Holland finally won its independence from Spain.
The Frondes in France. This was a revolt of the nobles and middle-class against the unpopular regent Ann of Austria and her Minister Mazarin.

1649 Execution of Charles I of England.

1652 The Protestant English started a war against the Protestant Dutch. Bitter rivalries had grown up between the two countries over fishing rights, trade and colonies.

1653 Oliver Cromwell became Lord Protector of England.

1658 Cromwell died.

1660 In England the rule of Parliament ended. Charles II, the son of Charles I, returned to England amid great rejoicing.

1661 Louis XIV came of age and began his long reign.

Famous people

1665 Plague spreads through London.

1666 The Great Fire of London.

1667 During the Second English War against the Dutch, a fleet under the Dutch Admiral De Reuter sailed up the Thames and the Medway and burnt a number of warships.

1670 Charles II signed the secret Treaty of Dover with Louis XIV. In return for badly needed money, Charles agreed to support Louis against the Dutch.

1672 The Third Dutch War. Under the Treaty of Dover England was allied with France against the Dutch.

1679 Because it disliked Catholics, Parliament passed a bill to exclude the King's brother James, a suspected Catholic, from the throne.

1683 Death of Colbert, for twenty years Louis XIV's Minister of Finance.

1685 James, Duke of York, becomes King of England on the death of his brother Charles II.
Louis XIV disliked the Huguenots (French Protestants) and drove about 200,000 out of France.

1688 James II was forced to give up the throne of England. He had favoured Catholics in the government, army and Church. William of Orange and his wife Mary (daughter of James II) were invited to succeed James as William III and Mary II.

1694 Queen Mary II died.

1700 Death of King Charles II of Spain. Louis XIV claimed the throne of Spain for France, starting a European war which lasted until 1714.

1702 Death of William III. He was succeeded by Queen Anne.

Anne (1665–1714) was Queen of England and the last of the Stuart line. A very ordinary woman, Anne succeeded William III, the husband of her childless sister Mary. During her reign (1702–1714) Britain's empire grew rapidly.

Anne of Austria (1601–66) was the mother of Louis XIV. After the death of her husband, Louis XIII, in 1643, Ann became Regent of France. She was helped by an outstanding minister, Mazarin.

Charles I (1600–49) was unable to keep out of foreign quarrels or to solve his problems at home in England. By 1640 he was quarrelling bitterly with Parliament. Both sides went to war in 1642. Charles's army was defeated in 1645 and he was beheaded in 1649.

Charles II (1630–85) fled from England after the defeat of the Royalist army at Worcester in 1651. He returned to great celebrations in 1660 when it was clear there was nobody to follow Cromwell. All his reign Charles tried to avoid another civil war.

Colbert (1619–83) was Louis XIV's great financial minister. He created the wealth that Louis XIV spent on wars, Versailles and a lavish court.

Cromwell (1599–1658) was an enemy of Charles I. Oliver Cromwell first became leader of Parliament's New Model Army in the Civil War and then became ruler of the country. He was the first uncrowned ruler of England.

Galileo Galilei (1564–1642) built one of the first telescopes in 1609. He was a great Italian scientist, but because the Catholic Church thought his ideas about the universe were too dangerous and unsettling he was put on trial for heresy. To save his life he agreed that his ideas were misleading.

William Harvey (1578–1657) showed how blood circulates through the body by examining the hearts of animals. His discovery marks the beginning of modern medicine.

Henrietta Maria (1609–69) was the sister of Louis XIII, the wife of Charles I and mother of Charles II and James II. She was disliked in England as she was both a Roman Catholic and pro-French.

James I (1566–1625) was the son of Mary Queen of Scots, beheaded by her cousin Queen Elizabeth I in 1587. James was already King of Scotland when he succeeded to the English throne in 1603.

James II (1633–1701) was disliked because it was believed he was a secret Catholic. When he came to the throne after his brother Charles's death in 1685 he showed great favouritism to Catholics. He was allowed to flee in 1688.

Johann Kepler (1571–1630) believed that the sun, not the earth, was at the centre of the universe. After many years of patient work, Kepler also showed that the planets did not orbit the sun, but travelled around it in elipses.

Louis XIV (1638–1715) was King of France and the most powerful ruler in Europe. The years of his reign are known as 'Le Grand Siècle' (The Great Century). Under him France led the western world in art, architecture and literature. Until constant wars ruined the country, it was also very rich.

Mary II (1662–94) was cursed by her father James II after he had fled from England and she and her husband, William, became King and Queen of England. She was very popular.

Sir Isaac Newton (1642–1727) was one of England's greatest scientific geniuses. He discovered the laws of gravitation and of bodies in motion. This helped explain why the stars and planets stay in the sky.

Rembrandt van Rijn (1609–69) was one of the greatest artists of all times. Rembrandt was Dutch, a brilliant drawer and a wonderful portrait painter.

Richelieu (1585–1642) was one of the great ministers of France. From 1624 until his death Cardinal Richelieu served Louis XIII. His greatest work was to destroy the power of the French nobles, so increasing the King's power.

George Villiers, 1st Duke of Buckingham (1592–1628) was the favourite of James I and then Charles I. He rose rapidly to fame and fortune after 1618. Hated by the King's enemies in Parliament, he was assassinated in 1628.

William III (1650–1702) was married to James II's Protestant daughter Mary. He was a great Dutch war-leader and a Protestant. He was, therefore, a very suitable person to become King of England. He agreed to work with Parliament and not against it. He spent most of his reign fighting wars against Louis XIV.

Sir Christopher Wren (1632–1723) was the famous English architect who rebuilt St Paul's Cathedral and many City churches after the Fire of London.

Glossary

carnival The season of festivities before Lent – the forty days of fasting ordered by the Church from Ash Wednesday to Easter.

doublet A man's short, close-fitting jacket. A doublet could have sleeves or be sleeveless.

dyke A wall built to keep the sea from flooding the land, or a large ditch or canal dug to drain marshy land.

flax A plant with a long stem and blue flower. Its fibres are used for making linen.

Huguenot A French Protestant (*see* Protestant).

intendant An important servant of the king in France, Spain and Portugal, who was given great power.

linen A cloth made from threads spun from flax. A very common material before cotton was widely used.

masque A play or entertainment where the actors hid their faces with masks.

Protestant A member of one of the churches led by those reformers (such as Luther, Calvin, Zwingli) who disagreed with the practices of the Catholic Church. In England extreme Protestants were often called 'Puritans' because they wanted to 'purify' the English Church of all Roman Catholic practices and beliefs.

rack An instrument of torture on which a victim's body was stretched in order to make them confess a crime.

reform To improve or to change for the better things that are unsatisfactory, wrong or evil.

Renaissance A French word which means re-birth. It is used to describe the great interest people in the 15th and 16th centuries showed in the ancient Greeks and Romans.

Index